# Craft Show Success

## The Artisans' Guide
## to Sales

C. A. Manestar

# TABLE OF CONTENTS

# A Quick Introduction

Hello, fellow Crafter!

I've been successfully working Craft Shows for 25 years. Part time or full time, it's a great way to meet new friends, and I'm always excited about the next show. This book is written for those artisans and crafters who do Craft Shows, Fairs and Festivals. Although the shows have changed little since the 1990's, the information and way these events are run, researched and advertised have changed drastically. Some of the biggest changes have come in the 2000's with Facebook, Twitter etc. The information in this book is targeted to help both new and established vendors. Much of the information here will help you consider different ways to reach your destination - a successful and profitable show.

I believe that when people are successful at these shows, we all profit. The shows I love the most are full of happy, busy vendors and enchanted buyers. That magic combination of talented people and excited customers is what keeps me going. I hope you'll use this book as one of your important tools, discover some new ideas, and get inspired.

Let's all do well together.

Regards,

Colleen aka ClockworkZero

C.A. Manestar

# PART ONE: To Show or Not to Show

In Part One we're going to jump right in and help you start at the beginning - analyzing your craft show; we'll discuss how to determine which shows will suit *your* business.

Let's start by investigating the shows: where to find them, how to judge if a new show is worthwhile, and how shows have changed over the years. What should you know before applying? Most importantly - how to accurately determine the costs of each show.

Be warned, there will be some arithmetic!

# Research the Show

Thousands of Craft Shows take place across the country every year, driving an economy of artisans and craftspeople. I'm certain no one really knows just how much money changes hands in this primarily underground marketplace. Some shows are well organized businesses with professional vendors, but a greater majority of shows are locally run, more amateur, smaller affairs.

No matter which type of show you are doing, you have to know if it will be worth your time and effort.

In the past, shows were advertised primarily in area newspapers or bulletins. Now most shows advertise online on their personal websites, or on aggregated sites that provide you with listings of shows. You can subscribe to some sites and they will email you local listings, or you can search through listings geographically at sites such as www.festivalnet.com. Festival Net is great because it covers both Canada and the US, and tells you if the shows are juried, offer prizes, and the number of vendors accepted.

Many of these sites still won't cover smaller local shows though, so you should look at virtual Community Bulletin Boards like Craigslist (www.cragslist.com). Craigslist has a large community section, and events often show up under the category of Artists or Events. Look for old listings of shows you might have missed. Most listings expire after 3 months or less, but after the Christmas season I frequently go through and consider some of the shows I didn't attend and put them on a list for the next season.

Some organizers will do 2-3 shows a year, so even if there isn't a show in the next month, or if the listings have expired, I still send them an email asking to be added to their vendor list for the next season.

Look for Facebook pages of last year's shows which can give you an idea of the venue, layout and lighting. Some shows will have write-ups online, articles or blog pages. If vendor lists are available I will often 'check out' the other vendors. It gives me an idea of what quality of vendors were at the show, if my work would fit with the rest, and possibly a profile of the customers. One of my favorite shows, The Bazaar of the Bizarre, has an 'alternative' theme. It is a craft show, as they claim, by "independent makers of all things exotic, whimsical and macabre." Most of the customers are looking for odd, unusual gifts or personal items. Knowing the customers' expectations allows me to create certain items that fit that market. I don't want to sell rhinestone dog collars at a cat show.

If it's possible to attend a particular craft show before you apply, you must take that opportunity. Many shows will have Spring and Winter versions. Some well established shows will run repeatedly for years, and it is important to track these shows and their application times.

Begin a list of shows and continue your research. Does the show have a webpage and is it up to date? Do they have photos of their previous shows? Some show photos could give you an idea of how busy the show might be, while other photos seem devoid of anyone but the vendors.

Once you have a few shows you are considering doing, it's

time to determine if these shows will be right for you and your products.

# Location, Location, Location

If you live in or near an urban center, you likely have the greatest variety of craft shows. Much of this information focuses on small to mid-range shows, but it can be applied to farmers markets, art shows, and flea markets, in places ranging from the local church basement to arenas and convention centers. In the summer there are outdoor shows in parks, at community centers, and schools. There are many opportunities for a vendor, but that doesn't mean you have to sign up for every show.

Start by reviewing the location of a show. Even if you've done the show in the same location before - circumstances change. I've signed up for shows at familiar locations only to discover the street had been under construction for two months. A few moments of research can help you determine if this show will be a good place for your customers.

Many of the aspects of a "brick and mortar" shop can be applied to craft shows: is there parking nearby, what are the hours of operation, is there lighting and electricity provided, what is the neighborhood like?

Before I apply for a show I use Google Maps and review the area. If I can't reach it easily, I won't attend the show. You might be willing and able to travel, but will your customers? If parking is limited or non-existent then you have to look at transit options. I once did a show that turned out to involve a three hour return trip from a remote location. While the table fees were low, the travel costs took too large a percentage of the profits.

Look for the "Walk Score" of the immediate area around the show. The walk scoring system is frequently used by real estate sites to help you figure out if you want to live in that neighborhood. Walk Score sites typically covers transit, if people can "walk to the shops", local attractions and parking. Some sites even let you know if the area is high in certain crimes. Living in a big city isn't always safe, and I know one vendor at a Gem Show who was mugged in the parking lot in a rough area of town. The show organizer moved the event the following year.

Consider what other attractions are in the area that might draw in customers. Once you've been accepted into the show, do ask the organizers if there will be local advertising like posters or signs to draw people to the show. It's always disappointing to get to a show and realize there is nothing indicating the show is happening.

# What's the Attraction?

Some craft shows may have run for years and are well known, established events within their area. North America's, "One of a Kind Show" brings talented vendors from across the country, and customers by the tens of thousands. Even when I first worked there helping a vendor at the show in 1991, it was well promoted and focused on unique and high quality crafts.

Most cities support a few well known shows and the competition to get into them can be fierce and expensive, because they can deliver the what customers want: high quality, unique art and crafts. For vendors, these shows deliver the customers. All shows need to advertise, so I often question if I'll do a show if they don't seem to do any advertising beyond a Facebook page.

Smaller shows though can still provide vendors with the numbers of customers they need. Shows that are often more successful have some kind of target shows or themes, or are part of larger events. Science Fiction or Comic Book Conventions are great examples of such events because they take vendors that compliment their themes.

Finding a show focused on a segment of customers can improve your success. Customers who like pottery or sewn items might go out of their way to attend a show themed for them.

# Evaluating Your Show Cost

Craft Shows are worth my time because they're fun and *always* profitable.  Fun, because I've made fantastic friends at these events: both vendors and customers.  Profitable? Yes.  I've seen the challenges many vendors experience with the second part of that statement.  I've seen too many vendors leave the show quietly dejected or complaining loudly.

What went wrong?  Wouldn't it be great to know if a Craft Show is going to be worth your time before you even apply?

Here's what I do: I sit down and work out some basic numbers. I'm a bit math phobic, so the "numbers" I calculate are simple.  Sure, this won't tell me if the show might be a flop because of a hurricane, but it will allow me to calculate the risk.  Every venture comes with some risk.

First consider your Show Cost, and then break that down into an hourly goal.

Show Fees + Show Expenses = **Show Cost**

**Show Cost** divided by **Number of Hours** = **Basic Show Cost per hour**

Table fees can start around $60 in urban areas and the hours vary.  Yes, some shows are a lot more, and in some cities, that $60 might only buy you a four foot table in the far back corner, but the formula still applies.  Many shows run about 6-7 hours, but you will likely need to factor in at least one hour for travel time.  I always allocate an extra hour even if the show is in my neighborhood because it covers my time to pack and return. So let's imagine you heard about a 6 hour show where the table fees are only $80.

$80 (show fee) + $40 expenses (travel, parking, etc) =$120

Now we know your show cost is, *at the least*, $120. Can you sell $120 worth of product? Do you have enough to sell to cover that and more?

Once I've got the basic cost, I start breaking it down into the number of hours. My mind is happier with smaller numbers. As well, if it is a very short show, the sales needed to cover that cost per hour will be high.

Show Cost - $120 divided by 7 work hours = $17.14 per hour.

This means that *nearly* the first $20 sold every hour will go directly towards paying these costs.

You need to make sure that you sell a lot more than that $17.14 an hour, so that you will make a profit with your sales. If you know your average sales from previous shows, you can decide how easily it will be to reach that basic figure. If you're launching a new product or you've only done a few shows, you can at least guess at how many products you will need to sell to cover the very basic cost.

The longer the show, the more commitment you need, and the higher the costs, not just in fees. Most people will need hire help so wages have to be factored in as a Show Expense.

Longer shows give you more time to sell, but shows that run beyond five days require a lot of product and time. I once was hired to help at a 3 week show. The vendor who employed me did nearly half his yearly sales in those 3 weeks. He would often sit down and "do the numbers" so that he could tell his staff, exactly the figures they needed to sell in order for him to make a profit. It was extremely motivating when he offered us a bonus based on his calculations.

The fees, the value of my time, and the cost of putting my art on the table are the biggest factors I review before I consider applying for the show. So, what are these fees all about?

# Show Fees

When I first started doing shows I imagined the organizers were lining their pockets with the table fees. Where was the money going? Why were some shows $40 for a table and others were $120? Before long I realized an organizer had a lot to handle: the venue, flyers, rented tables, countless emails, phone calls and queries. Whew! Just thinking of handling all those issues gives me pause. There's a ton of work that goes into every show, and the fees make up a large chunk of the expenses.

Some shows fees are extremely high. Toronto's premier craft show has booths that start around $2,000 for their smaller Spring show. The application process is daunting: amazing photos required, well written descriptions and artist statements are a must. There are lots of restrictions, and the hours are long. The competition for a spot top shows is like a contest where the winners get to work until they drop.

So what should your show fees get you? Customers. Hopefully lots of customers, because the greater the number of customers the greater your chance to make a sale.

If the cost of the show seems very high, chances are the attendance reflects those fees. Some shows with high booth fees also charge admission. I'm usually wary of shows with admission fees, because they need to have a large enough advertising budget in order to get people to spend their money before they've entered the show. Personally, I'm no fan of paying an admission fee unless I know there's going to be some amazing art there. You have to review these shows carefully. I've traveled the country doing such shows, and during the Winter season, a bad snowstorm can ruin a vendor's high hopes.

It ought to be quite obvious where your fees are going. Larger shows will take out print media advertisements as well as radio and online ads. If you can't figure out why a show's fees are high, ask them about their expected attendance.

If you know any of the vendors from the previous show, take a minute to ask them about their experience. Many vendors are quite approachable, even if they feel you might be in competition with their product.

If you are part of a craft community (for example, Etsy.com has some great local communities with Facebook pages) ask if anyone has information about the show. "Has anyone done XYZ show?" What did they think of the advertising and what was the attendance like? You might be surprised at the feedback.

One thing to consider: most shows, big or small, will not refund your fees. Once you've made a payment, it is rare to get your money back for a cancellation, even if your dog ate all your sock monkeys. It seems unfair, but the show has to go on - with or without you!

Sadly, the fees aren't everything you need to worry about, because there's other costs too.

## **Hidden Costs**

Now that you've decided to do the show, you start to fill out the application and guess what?  You've missed a bunch of costs that weren't evident when you first heard about the show.  You might get a detailed form or application to return with your fees. And surprise! You discover that $60 table fee didn't mention you have to rent a chair for $5.

One cost I frequently overlook is a "Processing Fee" or "Application Fee".  Not only do you have to pay for the table, you have to pay to apply to the show.

Some shows still require actual photos or portfolios of your work.  So although there's no application fee, you need to pay money to send in a portfolio or get photos or worse - CDs! Thank goodness for the internet, since now most shows accept virtual photos.

Well managed shows will tell you these costs up-front in the application (one chair provided, extra chair = $10), and some will only let you know when you go to submit your payment. I know one show that requires a credit card and some that want a "security deposit".

Some shows will charge for extras like lighting, power, Wi-Fi, credit card processing, security as well as booth rental.  I've been to shows where you cannot leave the booth without asking the security to "booth sit" - which was an extra fee that came off your deposit.  Some shows ask the vendors to put up local posters - which have to be picked up and distributed.  Those hours distributing flyers should be factored into your "cost of the show".

Review the fine print carefully before you send in your money.  Once you know the fees, you can start looking at ways to save.

Some costs can be minimized.  Can I bring my own chair or tent?  Can I use my own credit card system ?  If the show is not too far can I take public transit.  Perhaps you can avoid parking at the event by getting a ride.

Transportation can be expensive which is why many shows only feature local artists.  These costs of course increase for out of town shows, which might include accommodation costs, local transit costs, meals and shipping.

Budget for a meal and a drink even if you bring it from home.

So despite all the fees and costs, you've got a hundred fluffy bunnies you spent the Winter making, and the Craft Show is still the place to sell them.  Although that might sound a bit like a joke, I usually spend January and February rebuilding my depleted robot army, waiting for the shows to begin.

## **Tracking Your Shows and Applications**

Google offers an excellent Calendar, but there are many apps available that will help you stay organized. I talked to some vendors who do thirty or more shows a year, making it a full-time job.

As I come across various shows I will enter information into the Calendar - and if I can find out when they are taking applications I will make a note. Virtual calendars will send you a reminder of when your application is due, as well as an e-mail reminder about the show.

Of course new shows are always popping up in the bigger cities, so it is important to join up with communities or Facebook pages where these shows advertise. Etsy.com has a lot of communities you can join as long as you have an Etsy account.

Occasionally I will see flyers or posters for shows that I never heard about before. I'll snap a photo with my phone, or write down the information for next time. If I can figure out who to e-mail, I'll send them a note asking if I can be added to their vendor application list for their next show.

Once you've chosen the shows you want to attend, filled out the applications, and gotten the results, you need to ensure that you keep an eye out for the responses.

Use your calendar to schedule the following reminders and notes:

1. Show name, application deadline, requirements.

2. Reminder for application sent out a few days before the due date.

3. Expected response date.

4. If accepted: payment date

5. Show date.

6. Set-up time.

And now, finally, once I've picked the show, applied, been accepted, sent off my fees, it's time to set myself some target goals.

## PART TWO:  The Big 3 Targets

Huzzah!  You've sent off your fees and in a few weeks or months you'll be ready for the show day.

How many products would you *like* bring to your show? Thousands! How many products can you make and sell? Fifty or sixty!  Will that be enough?  Only one real way to know...

Time for more math.

In this section we're going to work though the example with my imaginary friend, Oliver.  Even if you don't like the idea of targets, Part Two will help you figure out how to determine how much you need to sell to make a greater profit.

# **Target One: Covering the Show**

Oliver the vendor goes to a Craft Show with sixteen sock monkeys. Each monkey sells for $30. The time he will spend at the is 8 hours. The Show Costs are $120 including expenses like gas for his motorcycle and a sandwich for lunch. If each monkey costs $10 to make, how many monkeys does Oliver need to sell to cover his cost? More importantly, how many monkeys does Oliver need to sell to buy enough pizza for his friends who had to endure endless discussions about sock monkeys*?

Arithmetic!

Seriously, it's a great idea to set up some targets so you know where to shoot.

How many of your products do you need to sell to pay the Show Costs? What do you need to sell to cover the production costs? How many sock monkeys need to sell for Oliver to make pizza money? We'll start with that equation we in section one: Show Cost! We'll pretend that Oliver already worked out the show cost to be $120.

Let's start with figuring out how many products Oliver needs to sell to cover the show cost.

Show Costs: $120 / Average item price $30 = 4 items

Sitting in his room, surrounded by Sock Monkeys, Oliver thinks at first he will only need to sell a few to cover the show costs. But then he realizes, if he sells 4 monkeys at $30 each he'll cover the cost of the show, but he still won't cover the cost to make those 4 products. He needs to do both.

Oliver's cost to produce a monkey, given how fast he sews, and that he's using his old socks for material, is $10. There's a section later in the book to help you figure this out... later. Right now we're setting up our first goal. Instead of using his sales price he's going to use his profits - that $20 (sale price minus costs).

$120 / $20 = 6

So Oliver has to sell 6 monkeys in total to cover the show costs. This is going to be Target One

6 products x $30 = $180.

Now we have our first target: $180.

How many items do you need to sell to cover your own costs? I usually sell a mix of products: a few cufflinks, a few necklaces and perhaps a few earrings. Since I started tracking my sales I figured out which products sell the best (necklaces followed by cufflinks, and finally earrings). Tracking what sells allows you to stock more of the popular product.

Now you've got one target set. In some ways, this goal is your closest. This target you should reach easily (and hopefully rapidly) because that just covers your basics. You, like Oliver, want some profits to buy pizza.

## **Target 2: Hourly Sales**

I like to set myself up with hourly targets. Small numbers seem much more achievable. Our friend Oliver is going to set some hourly goals.

Target One divided by Number of Show Hours = $180 (Show Costs) / 8 (hours) = $22.50 an hour.

You have a very basic target sales goal per hour. Take your average price of your item and divide your Show costs.

My average item sells for $40. I've got a few more expensive items and a few less, but most of the sales I make are in the $40 range. Chances are good, even with a disastrous show I can sell at least 4 or 5 items in 6 hours.

Most of the time I'll make a sale or two in the first hour. Depending on the layout of the show, and your location to the entrance, it might take a while for customers to arrive at your booth. I always get anxious if I have no sales in the first hour, so I make myself busy rearranging my items, making some show notes, or poking at some work I bring to finish.

Once the customers arrive, you can get focused and begin to hit the show targets.

## Target 3: The Bullseye

I have a friend that judges his show success on how much beer money he earns. For me its supplies and dinner. Can I buy that special chain I've mentally been fondling? Will tonight's dinner be Mac 'n Cheese or a fancy restaurant? Although a few vendor's I've spoken with have hard monetary goals ($500 of profit!), most vendors seem to prefer not to use such concrete numbers. Perhaps it's just easier than stressing ourselves out about money.

Even if you don't want to stress yourself with setting this goal, it will help you figure out how much you can potentially make at the show.

Regardless of what target number you are trying to reach you need to figure out how many sales will get you there.

Our friend, Oliver, ideally would like to bring home a $1000. That's a lot of pizza and a lot more sock monkeys than he has ready.

If he sells every monkey, he will have $480 in his pocket (16 monkeys @ $30). Take out the production costs ($10 per item): $480 - 160 = $320. Now remove the show costs. $320 - 120 = $200. So should he sell out, his maximum profit will be $200.

Although it's a long way from $1000, Oliver would be pretty happy to sell everything. $200 will buy pizza, new socks, etc. But is there a way he can make more?

Oliver realizes, after doing all these calculations, that there are ways to make more profit. There's a few monkeys with special costumes, the hooded guy with a bow and arrow alone is worth more. Oliver's prices need to get tweaked.

Oliver should also research his regional prices, and then he'll discover that the average price seems to be around $35. Yes, there are some people who's monkeys are well under $20. He's going to ignore them. In Part 3 we will be reviewing and discussing pricing.

Once Oliver's tweaked his pricing, he might also want to reconsider some costs. Instead of fancy packaging he might chose something less expensive. He might ask a friend for a lift to the show, and take the transit home. He won't buy food at the show, but take some apples and a snack. At this point, every penny he pinches will help increase the money he will earn.

Although I've done dozens of craft shows in the past few years, I've never sold everything at a show. I always have a surplus, even if it is very thin.

Still, without setting this target, I wouldn't know how much to bring. The bigger the show, the higher the goal.

If my goal for the show is $500 worth of sales I make sure I have at least $750 of merchandise. Usually I take about 50% extra. This way I can exceed the goal if the show is busy, still give my customers a selection and have extra stock for the next show.

How many items do you need to bring to hit the big target? Do you have enough to exceed your target or will you fall short because you just didn't bring enough?

Sometimes, these very basic equations will also allow you to judge if there is something off with your pricing.

If the number of items you need to sell is extremely high, in order to just cover the basic costs to do the show, then it is very likely you need to review your prices, which we'll deal with next.

* And.... how many monkeys does Oliver need to sell to buy enough pizza for his friends who had to endure endless discussions about sock monkeys?  Well, a lot more than our friend Oliver can make, alas!

# PART THREE:  Time and Money

Before we get into pricing and more money concerns, we're going to get a bit controversial.  Some people feel very strongly about what craftspeople and artisans should get paid.  Some vendors just don't pay themselves anything.  As you might guess, I believe we all should get paid fairly.

We're going to start with evaluating your time, and then look at some pricing strategies.

## **Pay yourself first.  Pay yourself well.**

My father always said, "Your time is valuable and you deserve to be paid for what you do."  It took me years to realize the value of this advice.  I'd started making jewelry as a hobby, squeezed into the time around my day job.  I'd make necklaces while watching TV at night.  I'd make them on the weekend.  If I sold some, I never calculated in a wage.  Wages were for people who were employed by a company not for someone sitting through a Game of Thrones marathon.  Why should I pay myself to watch reruns?

There seemed to be a lot of reasons not to pay myself a wage. And I could sell my work cheaper if I didn't pay myself.

But as my business grew, and I had to pay the show costs, I started to realize that it wasn't TV time any more. I was spending weekends creating jewelry and robots. 'Spare time' had become work time.

Part of figuring out a fair price is paying yourself.  A lot of people seem to disagree with artisans paying themselves for their work.

Would you expect someone to work for free every weekend and evening?  No.  Would you expect someone to work for $3.00 an hour when everyone else is being paid $20?  No.

When my Etsy store started making sales, I started doing Craft Shows again, and at some point in time, the hobby became a business. I needed to buy more materials, get packaging, provide business cards and, gee!, make sure I got paid for my time.

Try asking: Why do I want to do a Craft Show? Yes, there is the lure of money but you might already realize it isn't that easy to achieve. Is it a way to get feedback? Are you testing a new product line? Are you trying to build a local customer fan base?

For me the answer is primarily down to two aspects. First, I like to see people wearing or admiring my work. If it were only that, though, I would just give away my creations. The second factor is that I make money from my work.

I've always been able to turn a profit at Craft Shows. Even when the shows were terrible and there were only a few customers. Sometimes it was a very small profit, but it was profit over and above the booth fees, secondary costs and the actual materials. This might be in part due to the items I'm creating, but I know the largest factor is treating the event as a business.

Even if you only do a few shows a year you need make certain you are on the plus side of the equation, otherwise you'll become discouraged or quit. By figuring out the actual show costs, and a fair price for your work, you will be ahead of most vendors.

I read someplace that a business born out of love can still become a chore. I found, having run a few different businesses, that one of the fastest ways to sacrifice my love of what I am doing is to run it at a loss. Making certain I'm paid for my time helps me stay motivated on the long term.

So, yeah. Pay yourself well. You and your work are worth it.

# Pricing Your Work

Before you get too deep into these next few points, I would like to say that this is just one way to help you figure out the fair price for your products. There are many other ways to calculate pricing, but this is one of the ones I've used over many years. Even if you are happy with your prices, try working through the next few points to see what you get. Explore!

Price and profit are the hardest factors to assess whether you have been selling for decades or you have just begun vending. The price for your art is not fixed and may change over time. Generally, the cost of materials increases over time, and this should be reflected in your price.

On average I've noted about 25% of vendors at the shows I've seen seem to under-price their work. Having created jewelry for so many years I have a fairly good idea of the cost of designing a product, so when I see some of the prices, it isn't surprising to learn the vendors are either new to selling at craft shows, are trying to build a customer base and think that undercutting the competition will accomplish that , or haven't changed their prices in years.

You need to be objective about pricing your creations, which can be difficult when you are attached to your work. Some people have problems figuring out where to get started. I start with my 3 keys to pricing:

# The 3 Keys to Pricing

The following equation can help you work out a base price for your products:

Cost of Materials  +  Labor + Expenses = Price

The Cost of Materials *also* needs to include: packaging (the box or bag you present to your customer), and business cards.

Your Labor is an hourly wage, based on your local wages, and is the actual time you spend producing your item.

Expenses are, for me, the most difficult to calculate.  These are a bunch of costs, and will vary with your product.  Some might be minor:  sewing needles, thread, price tags, etc. While some can be much larger: studio rental fees, design courses, advertising costs.

Let's sit down with a big cup of coffee/tea/wine and figure these terms out in more detail.

## 1) The Cost of Materials

The Cost of Materials should include every material that goes into making and presenting your product to your customer. Everything, from the note paper you use to sketch out your drafts, to the tissue paper inside the box.  It includes your business cards too.

There's a lot of little things that get overlooked: price tags, gift tags, tape, the wrong kind of paint or glue. If you do casting it might be the cost for a mold or failed casts. Did you ever buy chain or varnish and find out it was the wrong type? Yes, those things too go into your costs.

Basically, if you've put your hand in your pocket, for your business, it will count in some way. You paid money out. Accounting for all your materials makes sure you get your money back.

## 2) Labor

Your Labor is an hourly wage. At the base you might start with your local wages but you need to increase that figure to account for the your skills and talent.

 I'm not much of a fan of basing it on local regional wages because in the online market I am competing with countries with much lower minimum wages. If you've spent years learning to produce your crafts as many silversmiths do, your hourly wage needs to reflect the fact that you are an expert.

An expert knitter might be able to produce a sweater in a matter of days. It takes me a year of weeping to produce a scarf. There is a lot of skill involved, and it takes time to learn to create your products. When you only pay yourself minimum wage or less you are doing yourself a disservice.

 Labor is the actual time you spend producing your item. It also includes the time you spent making a failed version of your product, or the time you had to repaint an item, or develop your prints.

I've seen arguments online where people claimed that "time is free"! What you do with your spare time is "free". It's as if there is a special rule that applies to craftspeople.

If I have to pay someone to help me make my jewelry I don't expect them to work for free. My business would pay them a wage. If I need a photographer I hire one. You are an employee of your business.

When I send in a design for a business card to get printed I don't question the printer when she tells me that a rush job costs $20 extra because she will have to stay late to print it. I don't tell her she should charge less because the minimum wage is only $11.00

Don't undervalue yourself. Paying yourself minimum wage doesn't account for the full value of what it takes to make your wonderful art and craft.

## 3) Expenses

As I mentioned, I often have trouble with figuring out my expenses. There's a lot of costs that are easy to overlook. I'm often terrible at remembering to count transportation as an expense, for example.

Once you start looking you might be shocked at all the expenses you accumulate that are needed to support your art. Big expenses, like getting a banner printed stand out. Small expenses like buying masking tape can get overlooked. Just try your best for now, to list as much as you can. Hopefully, as your business develops, you will get better at tracking.

Start writing down all your expenses. Big stuff: yes, that new printer, your monthly subscription to that Pottery website, business cards etc. Little stuff: tape and glues and solder, oh my.

Expenses need to be divided by the possible number of items you can produce in a given time.

Let's imagine a scenario....

## **Logan's Wood Carving**

I'm going to illustrate how your Expenses work.  Here's an example based on a woodworking artist I knew years ago. I'm going to change his product slightly, and call him Logan. We worked in a co-op gallery and over a few days we discussed art and pricing.  The figures here are simplified:

Logan's Monthly Expenses:

Studio fee:  $300
Transportation: $60
Heat/Hydro: $50
Office Supplies: $10
Advertising: $60
Specialty Tools*: $30
Training*: $15
Miscellaneous costs: $40

Monthly Total:  $565

* Although Logan had inherited some great carving tools, he was thinking of buying a lathe, which he saved for each month.

**Logan said he worked out the cost of some courses and spread that over years.  The special equipment he uses will last a few years, but isn't cheap.

Logan usually creates about 10 finished products a month. So taking that monthly total we divide it by the number of items he usually produces each month:

$ 565/ 10 = $56.50

Since he spends about 12 hours a week at his studio (including transit time) we know that those 10 items equate to 48 hours a month - or 4.8 hours to produce one item. After some consideration, he realized he also spends time photographing and doing a bit of marketing of his finished product. It was closer to 6 hours.

6 hours x Labor @ $15 an hour = $72

The cost of materials, Logan figured was around (on average) $20.

So finally we get down to:

Materials = $20 + Labor = $72  Expenses = $56.50  for a total of $148.50.

Which sounds pretty expensive to some people - but he sells his work in galleries and at Big Craft Shows. His actual price though was around $300 for his products. The difference between that $148.50 and his $300 is nearly double.

Logan admitted he really had problems at first pricing his work so high. In fact, when he started he based his price on just the materials and "threw in a few dollars for my time". It was only when he had made a lot of sales he realized that he wasn't making enough.

Now if you've done all the above figures you might find out your prices are off. Let's look at finding a Fair Price.

# What's a Fair Price for Your Product?

So, you've worked out your own prices using the formula:
Cost of Materials  +  Labor + Expenses = Product Cost.

Did you just faint?  I did the first time I sat down and "did the numbers".  That cost put my price too high above my competitors, and was more than I expected anyone to pay. My materials were too expensive and I took a long time to make my work.

Does this mean you must change your pricing completely or give up making your crafts?  No.

I like to think that a Fair Price is a better term.  If the world were a fair place, you might get more recognition of your time, and the value of being an artisan. Figuring out the fair price means figuring out what the customers will pay and what you can afford to charge them.

Not all the customers can afford a $300 wood carving.  Most artists I know can't.  But Logan taught me that it is better to sell two sculptures a month (which was his average) then to try and sell 10 pieces at $60.   He said for a while he charged less, but it became unsustainable.

What you can also do is examine the pricing formula.   There are usually ways you can decrease your expenses.

Many years ago I realized one great way to save is to buy in bulk.  This meant a higher initial cost: buying 10 gift boxes at $2.00 was something I could afford right now.  Buying 100 gift boxes for $50 made sense, but sometimes I didn't have that $50.  I had to save up for it.  Then, a few weeks later I was back buying my 10 boxes, and there was a woman looking at the same boxes. A five minute conversation led us to buying the larger amount and splitting up the case outside the store. After that, I found better deals, and started buying as much as I could in bulk.

Consider the areas where you can reduce your costs:

- Can you share your studio costs?
- Is there a faster way to produce your products?
- Can you hire someone to assist in some aspect of your production?
- What items can be purchased in bulk? Is there another vendor or person who can share the cost of bulk purchases?

Once you have a Cost, see if there is a way to get that to a Fair Price, without shortchanging yourself. You might need to reduce or increase your profit margin a bit, if you feel that the Price is too high or too low.

Do have a look at the upcoming section on "perceived value", which can help you figure out where to price your work, but before you do, let's look at profit.

# Figuring out Profit in your Prices

If you have worked through the pricing scenario in the previous section it ended with my friend doubling the final cost of his product.

That big difference between what it costs to produce his work and the mark-up is his profit.  The difference allowed him to put his items on sale, and also offer wholesale prices to the galleries.

His mark-up also means he can sell fewer items at a show and still make a profit.  It gives him a budget for tools and future courses to improve his skills or buy new materials.

Reviewing these aspects of your pricing on a regular basis will allow you to stay competitive and pay yourself well.

Some people suggest doubling  the cost you figured out above:

Cost of Materials  +  Labor + Expenses = Cost x 2 = Sale Price

Personally, I think this works better for some items than it does for others.  I don't wholesale my work at this time, so the prices I offer to my customers is closer to the wholesale price.  As well, by simply doubling the price, your labor cost is twice what it was!

If you aren't happy using the above calculation, I would suggest you try:

(Cost of Materials  + Expenses) x 2 = Price A

Price A + Labor =  Sales Price

That formula worked much better for me, personally.  The figures I came up with were quite close to my pricing now.

I still do review what people are charging, and sometimes I will tweak my prices.

Review your prices, at least twice a year.  When I started making Steam-punk Jewelry the cost of buying supplies was much lower.  As it became popular, some of the material costs went up 100%.  What I bought six years ago for $1 is now $10, and scarcity has led to even greater increases.

If my prices don't change to reflect the increase in my materials, my profits go down.  If they go down too far, I will no longer be able to afford to make my designs because I can't replace the material.

# Perceived Value

Once in a while, I will meet a vendor whose prices appear shockingly high compared to similar items that are for sale. Did they over-priced their goods because they don't understand the market? Maybe the materials costs are very high, or they feel their work deserves the big price tag?

Sometimes a vendor will be so enamored to their own work they price based on their personal emotional attachment. I know I've made a few things I want to keep, but that feeling fades after a while. Sell your darlings! Make new ones...

But some vendors have figured out that the price of their items can be on the higher end of the scale if their customers believe the price reflects good value. If you suspect you've been undercharging for your work, this is a great chance to re-evaluate your price. One of the ways to increase the price of your product is to let your customers know why YOUR product is special. Remember, prices can always be discounted later.

Let's run through an example: why do people pay some incredible prices for name-brand running shoes? Are the multinationals truly producing the best shoes on the market, the most fashionable, or are they made of special rubber mixed with gold dust? Regardless of your answer, there are thousands of buyers who believe that certain design elements, styles, or materials create a superior product - and they will pay big bucks for those special shoes.

So you and I aren't multinationals; we don't have big budgets or perhaps any advertising budget. What we need to do on a much more intimate scale is to ensure that our customers know why our original design, style, and materials make our products desirable and excellent value.

What are the unique features? Make a list of ten or more aspects of your creation that make it different from similar items. An example of this might be the materials you use: are they recycled, rare or unusual? Where did you get your ideas? What was your inspiration?

Write. It. Down. The act of writing engages a different part of your brain then just reading words. Yes, you can bookmark this section to stop and write your notes and then come back later, just don't forget. (I know, I don't usually do those exercises in books, but when I do, they're usually worth it!).

Once you've determined some of the important or unusual features, you need to start to think of easy and clever ways to quickly tell your customers about them. "Easy ways", because you will need to repeat them and "quickly" so you can grab people's attention as they are walking by. You need to draw the customer's eyes to your wonderful products. Of course, you will tell them about it by talking to them, but this can get a bit exhausting, so one of the best tools is with signage. We'll be looking at different ways to design your signs later in the book.

Once someone is close enough to your booth or table, take a moment to give them more details. Tell them the interesting features and they will begin to understand what makes your work special and worth more than those across the room.

# **Overpricing**

Guessing your costs of production can be one of the main factors that lead to over or under pricing your product.

There's a few other factors which can lead to over-pricing. Sometimes we miscalculate our labor costs. Occasionally, it takes me a long time to make one particular item, far longer than it should. Like my failed attempts to knit - I would need to price that scarf at a thousand dollars to pay for my time. When you are learning to create something, you have to allow that you are unskilled, and cannot pay yourself an expert's wages. Skills take time to build, and apprentices just don't get paid as much.

Often, material costs can spin out of control. At that point you might realize that you can't afford your studio, and you have to do your work at home.

Some artists I know say it's quite difficult to detach themselves from their work. They are looking for the "right customer" who will understand their passion. They know there are people who pay thousands for art - and typically, most Craft Shows might not be a good place for such works.

# **Under-pricing**

There are a few things that lead to under-priced work. If someone has never worked out their costs, they often undervalue it. They might leave out one of those 3 key pieces when they calculate their price. They guess at their material costs, or they don't count packaging or business cards. They ignore their labor: they don't pay themselves much or at all. They forget miscellaneous expenses.

Sometimes they don't know what their local competitive prices are, and search online to try and figure it out. They find someone with a similar product, perhaps over in another country, and use that as their guide. They found the lowest price possible.

You cannot compete with factory prices because you aren't a machine. So far, all my attempts at getting my robots to self-replicate have failed!

Low prices don't equate to higher sales. Low prices can actually hurt your sales, because frequently, people think there is something wrong with your product and won't buy it. They might question why it is so inexpensive, or if you actually created it.

Personally, given the time it takes for me to make my jewelry, and the increasing cost of materials, (which have to be replaced), I would rather sell fewer items at a higher price than more at a lower price.

# Part 4:  Pre-Show Prep

Well, we have made our products, registered for the shows, figured out our pricing... it is almost time to get going!  I know I am often so busy making robots or jewelry that I don't have a lot of time to get ready for the actual event.

Even if you are a Craft Show Pro, you can always improve some aspect of your booth or signs, and minimize your set up time.  In this section we're going to discuss some ways to save you time, and hopefully improve your sales.

The more you plan ahead, the less your stress on the day of the show.

# **Trial Run**

Twice a year I do a test run of my booth, setting up the table and displays. It's a great way to rethink my designs and presentation. Sometimes I get dazzled by props I see at other shows, or in stores, or find some new way to display my wares.

Some vendors have incredible displays that take an hour or more to set up. I try and keep things portable, unbreakable and easy to set up.

Since I get to and from my shows without help, my biggest need is to ensure everything is portable. If I can't carry it, it isn't coming. I hope you might not have to consider transportation as much I do!

If you are a newbie to craft shows or you are introducing a new line of products, this is an opportunity to test it all out. Doing a new display the night before a show (or worse, at a show!) is too much stress.

Start by marking out the area you are allocated. Many tables are 2ft wide and 4ft or 6ft long. In the past I purchased folding tables of various lengths because some shows only supply tables for an extra fee. I use those to set up a few display options.

Snap a few photos of your display, move your items around and try new options. Don't forget: for every tweak you make, you should have a new photo, so you can check on what works later.

Although I rarely do outdoor shows, it is even more critical to nail down your set-up before hand when you are dealing with outdoor displays. Set up your tent on one nice, warm, non-show weekend.

Outdoor shows tend to expect you to bring your own tables, chairs and sunscreen, and sometimes the tent. I can't stress enough how important it is to do a trial run of your tent.

I once bought a tent the day before a craft show, when person who was going to lend me their tent discovered it was broken. It was incredibly stressful figuring it all out on the show day, in the wind and rain.

Once you've got a "booth" set up - take more photos. E-mail yourself a photo so that you can refer to it later. Review your photos on a laptop or desktop computer, because you will notice more detail instead of just looking at your display on your phone.

Once you are happy with the set up and display - you need to take a few great photos. Borrow or use a good camera!

Photos are quite important: they allow you to review the set up later, and perhaps poll friends to find out which set up they prefer.

Photos of your booth are often used in the submission process with bigger shows.

This is an opportunity for you to do a series of photos without the pressure of actually being at the show. If you can get some friends or family to pose as customers you can try and duplicate the feeling of being at a show. Have fun with your trial run! Pretend it is a photo shoot because these test run photos can be used a  reference and to advertise.

Photos you take should go up on your blog, any sites you have or even posted to communities.  If I  can I do  set-up photos of my outdoor arrangement, because the lighting is generally better.  I can hang signs, do the set up and have it all laid out.

Before you do your trial run, though, read through the next few sections for some tips.

# Condense table size

Since many shows charge more for larger tables, it is a great idea to plan for the smallest area you can manage. Store some products under the table, within easy reach. Keep all the bags, boxes and wrapping away from the tabletop. Invest in a tablecloth that will cover your table, almost to the floor at the front, but only hang down a foot or two at the back.

Vertical displays can work well to increase your available table space but be careful not to make them too high. Many vendors are hidden away behind their displays. You want your customers to see you, not just hear a voice emerging from behind a display.

I keep my displays simple because I usually take transit to my craft shows. Everything needs to fit in bags, and I have to be able to carry it. For some bigger shows or outdoor shows, I use folding tables and chairs. I purchased a tent on sale that packs down into a small, long box - that has wheels! Everything can fit inside the trunk of a taxi.

# Organizing Your Display

Too many items can dazzle and confuse your customers.

When I first launched a new product line of robots made of recycled hardware, I only had a dozen. I had almost twice the number by the next show and because each little robot was unique, some people would spend a long time deciding on which character they liked the best. Twenty minutes choosing an item under $40 is a long time if the show is busy. One customer told me that they just couldn't decide because there were too many choices.

Although it is tempting to have a lot of items on display it is often easier for a customer to chose one item from ten options (or less) then to pick out a single pair of earrings out of thirty. Hold the others in reserve, and restock the empty places.

Spacing your items out creates a sense of pattern and organization. In general, people like some kind of order: bracelets here and necklaces there.

Group your products by style or price if possible. If most hand-painted bowls are $10 on a table, keep the $20 bowls far away. It is always disappointing as a customer to think you are buying something for $10 to discover it is twice the price, so price stickers can help.

Many store displays will draw your focus to the more expensive items by isolating them. If you have some special items figure out a way to showcase them.

One vendor told me she arranges all her hand-knitted scarves by color as well as style. Visually this creates blocks of color in her displays. From a distance her booth feels organized. She said, "I only display about 25% of the scarves I bring. If I see someone is hesitant or digging through all the red scarves, searching, I will tell them I have a few additional selections put aside. I'll ask them if they are looking for a particular shade or style. Then I'll choose just a few to show them. 95% of the time I won't need to show them anything else." She feels that narrowing down the choices creates a better experience and gives her a chance to talk to her customers.

# The Display Game

Here's the game I like to play: Use Google Images to discover new displays.

Google up your own personal variation of your product category (ie: jewelry, sock monkeys, wood sculptures) and the words "craft show booth".  You could also use "art show booths" or "Farmers Market" etc.  You can variations like, "interesting jewelry craft show" or "pottery display craft shows".

You should get a variety of images from different craft shows.  Some look like disasters, some look so pretty they might be made by fairies and magic dust.

Can you figure out at a glance what they are selling?  Are the items hidden by the displays?  Are the displays more interesting then the products?

Try and see what works as a display, and if you can, disregard the color and ignore the product.

When I did this for jewelry I soon realized: earrings on "cards" worked better then earrings on a stand.  They are small items, and disappeared into the background unless they had some kind of backing.  They were visible from a few feet away - the cards made them stand out.

Analyze what makes the display work. Look at the spacing, the arrangement of the products, and signs or photos. After

I've found several images of craft show displays I saved them and sketched out a few alternatives.

You can also look at the images that you disliked. What didn't work? Were there too many items? Figuring out what doesn't work can help you understand what draws people to your display, or makes them pass you by.

Sometimes we need to set aside our personal preferences as well. I often personally prefer dark colors that offset my products, but some displays work well with brighter colors. Dark green might work for Oliver's products, but do some tests if you plan on working with bright colors. Solid, non-patterned tablecloths are a good choice, and don't restrict you to seasonal themes.

# What's for Sale?

I've seen vendors with coffee cups, food wrappers, snacks and foreign business cards on their table. Have a garbage bag under the table and use it.

I've seen some vendors who will include a bowl of candies, a vase of flowers and once, a bunch of balloons as part of their display. Between signs, prices, items for sale and your display, it can end up looking like the aftermath of a party.

Too many decorations can overwhelm your display. Your display should never detract from your product.

If people ask the price of a part of your display versus what you are selling, then it is time to look for another display, unless you really want to sell off your vintage suitcase. It might be fine if you have one person ask on the rare occasion, but if you have one or more person asking per show, you need to make some changes.

It should be clear from several feet away what is for sale. In some shows the isles are wide, which means you need to grab attention from farther away.

# Marketing: the Power of Signs

Billions of dollars are spent on advertising every year. Unfortunately, I've misplaced my billions, but I do think one of the cheaper ways to advertise is with signs. Over the last year, I've been working with a friend, William, who has taught me more about advertising and marketing than a hundred books ever could.

Signs don't have to be as large as your entire booth to grab attention. Many shows have restrictions on the type, style and size of your sign. Some vendors will have table signs with their company names, which is great if people are familiar with your company and product. Do my customers need to know my store name, ClockworkZero as they walk near or would they be more curious to explore what items I have if there's a sign saying, "The Robot Army"?

You don't always need a banner shouting at people or neon signs. You can get clever and create smaller, table top signs that can be seen from a distance of five or six feet.

Some of the best signs I've seen don't mention the name of the company, but instead focus on the selling features. Organic! Recycled! The customers are drawn into your space like curious cats.

When you are designing signs, I found spending a bit of money to get them professionally printed makes a difference. My local print shop offers stiff board stock paper which will last for years. Getting these signs printed for one particular show cost less than $20, and the signs will last until I want to change them.

Chose easy-to-read fonts in bright colors. My print shop called me and said they had a special font they thought would work even better than the ones I had chosen.

Do test signs and see if you can read them from a few feet away. Try different fonts. I print my test signs on my home printer before I email them to the print shop, so I have an idea of what I am buying.

# Part 5:  SHOW DAY

I love Show Day.  It is what we are all waiting for: that opportunity to meet new customers, sell our wares, find new treasures.

But wow, the stress!  The Pressure!

Let's see if there's ways to make our lives a little easier:

C.A. Manestar

# Check List for the Show

I've created a Check List of standard items to bring to the shows which is at the end of this book. I'm going to make it available as a free download as well, so that you can print it off if you've bought the paper book, or it should be a link if you are reading an e-book. Feel free to let me know if there are some big things missing, for the next edition.

In that Check List, you will see the first section, called "Craft Show Box/Bag".

Let's have a look at that Special Box of Stuff, first. I keep a box of items that travel to every show. That plastic, snap-lid box holds a lot of small items like duct tape, mirror, magnifying glass, an apron with many pockets which I commissioned specially for craft shows.

You might find you need some of the same items at every show, so why not store them all together? The items in one bag that never vary. Now don't be tempted to remove those items, because that is where it all falls apart. Don't let the family borrow from the box. Padlock it if you must.

My second bag contains variables, or items that need to be restocked more frequently, like: business cards, packaging, boxes, bubble wrap etc.

Go through the checklist at end of this book, because it can really save you time and sanity. I've also made it available for a free download at: www.finaldraftpress.com/camanestar

## <u>Visualize your Sales</u>

Before entering a boxing ring, running a race, or pole vaulting, athletes have been visualizing victories for many years. Before you get started on your day, spend a minute imagining your table layout, your favorite products all lined up and making your first sale.

So cue the Rocky music theme! My husband usually puts on some of my favorite music when I'm packing up, and even though I'm usually rushing around, it makes me smile.

Visualize selling all your items, and how happy you will be at the end of the day. It creates positive energy so when you get to the show you are already 'in the zone'.

# Be Comfortable

I debated putting this section into the book because it seems like common sense, but then, last winter I saw a vendor faint because she had "forgotten to eat". So don't forget to bring food and take a few minutes to eat. Standing around for hours, after spending the previous night packing, then rushing around on the morning of the show, will zap your energy. Energy bars are a good choice. Very few venues have access to a microwave, so stick to easy to eat items that won't leave crumbs!

I've also been to at least four shows over the years where a merchant has ended up ill from dehydration, so bring water. Outdoor venues are usually the hardest because of the weather and heat in the summer, so make sure you have some shade or protection from the elements.

Even if it's a 6 hour show, you should plan on standing around for 8 hours. Wear your most comfortable shoes!

One of the best tricks I've seen was a vendor who purchased an extra thick work-out mat, and stood on it all day. It rolled up, was lightweight and made a huge difference.

# **Be Early**

Plan to be at the show for the "Set Up" early, because there's a good chance you might get there late. If the show set up time is 9am until 10:30am - try to be there at 9am. Some shows won't allow you to set up too close to the opening hour. I've seen vendors arrive with boxes and bags at the last minute before the doors open, pushing their way in through the line ups, crying because their car broke down, or there was traffic, or they couldn't find a taxi.

Arriving late for the Set Up can cause a lot of chaos - not just for the vendor involved but for the rest of the vendors, the organizers, and sometimes even the customers.

I've seen vendors turned away by Organizers because they were late. Some Organizers are quite strict with their rules, and some applications outline the penalties, by stating that vendors will be turned away if they are late.

# **Part 6: Sales Tips**

Sales, sales, and more sales. We are all hopeful, but not always successful. We might disparage sales people, dislike them or admire them, but without sales your business withers. I've sold many, many different things: corn out of the back of a truck, plastic grid to build green driveways, Time Share packages, beads, websites, tee-shirts, graphics, and personalized Chinese stamps (seals). And of course I have sold robot sculptures, jewelry and whatever else I create.

I'm very, very good at selling. I also believe most people can do well, and we can all improve.

So now, it's time to put on your Selling Hat, and shine!

# The Number One Sales Person

I started thinking of myself, in the past few years, as an employee of my own business. You too might find you are a maker, photographer, web designer, advertiser, graphic designer, copy writer, organizer and sales person.

When I'm at the show I'm not only the artisan - I'm the best sales person the company could ever hire!

If you imagine you were hiring someone, and had to pay them $60 an hour, how would you expect them to look and act? Professional, knowledgeable, chipper or at least friendly. They'd wouldn't be preoccupied with a cell phone or book. You'd expect them to be ready to talk to every potential customer, because you are paying them $60 an hour! Sixty. Dollars. An hour. They wouldn't be hiding in the back, chatting with the vendor next door, slumped over or sitting down.

Well, if you've set yourself a goal of $60 in sales an hour, then you *are* that very expensive employee.

Think of all the times you've been annoyed at a sales person. Have you been irritated by someone who was too aggressive, too friendly, chewing gum or eating? Were they talking to their friends and ignoring you, the customer looking to buy? Or maybe you just couldn't find them.

Everyone has different points of annoyance with sales people. There are hundreds of sites that offer advice with

"Do's and Don'ts". Mostly, I just follow "figure out what bothers me with sales people - and don't do that!".

I do believe it is important to be enthusiastic about your own work. It can be difficult to display that emotion, and often after a show I'm drained. If you can share some of your passion, your ideas and inspiration honestly with customers they will respond.

## **Don't Judge**

Customers come in all sizes, shapes, income levels and ages. I try to acknowledge everyone, even if it might just be a nod or smile at someone passing my booth. You don't know who might be the person who will become a customer.

I've seen vendors making age judgments. Sometimes this comes out when they are making sales to children. Sometimes they will dismiss someone who is older than their average customer. Sigh.

You just don't know who will be your customer.

I personally learned this lesson because some children buy my work. In November I launched a trial of some new products made out of Vacuum Tubes and bits of hardware: Ray Guns! My personal jury was still out debating if they would be a permanent product, and I wasn't certain how to price them. Because of the materials and time involved I knew I wanted to charge at least $45 to $65 for them, in order to make a profit.

The first person to grab one was a boy, 9 years of age. He picked up the fanciest one, and I showed him the light on it, and told him it was $65 when he asked. We made some "pew-pew" noises and he wandered off. I didn't imagine that he would actually buy it.

Five minutes later he returned with a $100 bill. I asked to meet his mom or dad. His mom came over and confirmed all was fine.  Two months later she met me at a different show, and told me "it is his prized possession".  I never expected to sell it to someone so young, and certainly not at full price. Lesson learned.

Sometimes financial circumstances change for people too. When that customer who 'always buys something' at each show suddenly avoids your booth, try not to take it personally.  It likely has nothing to do with you or your crafts, but more to do with their finances.

## **Ignore the Ignorant**

Have you ever heard someone say, "Oh, I can make that!", or worse, "I can make that for half the price!".  How about, "I don't understand why this is so expensive.  It's just paper and glue and..."

Hearing these statements drives everyone who has ever created anything, absolutely crazy.  I've seen vendors flip out when they heard someone tell their child, "We don't need to buy that, we can make it at home."

Yes, perhaps they can make their own sock monkeys at home. Perhaps they can learn to knit, bead or sew.  But they aren't *doing* it.

Some people though say this to their children or each other because they can't afford your item. They aren't thinking about your feelings.  Since it is a bad business practice to shake them until their brains start working, ignore them.

Arguing with people about your prices, or your materials source, or your costs does not win you a customer.  Never get into arguments at a show.   I've seen it happen and everyone felt uncomfortable.

Ignore the ignorant.  Save your time, and energy for your customers.

One thing I should mention is that it is still okay to address problems.  A few times I've had people gather around the entrance of my booth or in front of my table, not to buy but to talk. I'll tolerate it for a few minutes, but if it seems to be a problem, I'll approach them and ask them to move. They forget they are standing in the "doorway" to my store, and have *always* been willing to move aside.

# **Tell them the story**

Every handmade item has a story to tell. What is the story of the work you have created? What were your inspirations, materials, ideas and themes?

Share the story of your work and you give your customers more than just a product.

People are more likely to buy an item, and to pay more for that item, when they feel a personal attachment. Your story should be simple and with a few key points the buyer can remember. My work is often created from pocket watch parts which date from 1890-1920. Often times this will be the only point the customer will remember later.

I also have a few key features of my products that I tell to people as they walk by. Talking to someone is an invitation to approach your table and find out more. It is better than saying hello, and draws people in.

Most customers at shows want to feel a connection to both the item and to the person who created it. They want to know YOU! Telling a good, simple story about how you got started, the materials you use, or aspects of your creative process will give your work that extra edge.

# Stand Up and Look them in the Eyes

Customers at a craft show love to meet the artist. Make sure you are clearly visible at all times and not hidden by your display.

Craft Shows can be exhausting, and sitting down is such a temptation. Don't sit down! It makes a huge difference if you are sitting when others are standing. It is easier to talk to your customers if you are standing because they are not looking down at you.

It can be difficult for many vendors to stand up for hours. Stools are a good option, but personally, if there is a potential client in the room I would avoid them as well.

When we walk down the street we tend to avoid looking directly at strangers because it creates a sense of connection, however temporary. But at the show people are there to meet you and view your work.

If you are shy, it can work well if you simply glance at them long enough to give them a brief smile or at least a nod. Always acknowledge their existence.

Invite them into a conversation with you by telling them a feature of your work. Ask questions. Many people don't know what a vacuum tube is - so I use it as a great opportunity to discuss the materials that make my robots.

# Up-selling

When I first was hired to sell goods at a craft show, I learned some of the biggest lessons on selling to the public.  Max, my old boss, taught me tips that I never forgot.  He was the master of up-selling his hand carved, Chinese stamps: The base models were $15.  The next size was only $20.00, but it was so much bigger!  Would they like an extra ink for $5.00, because they wouldn't be able to find it anywhere else?  How about a lovely custom box for $3.00, or would they like it in a paper bag?  On average his $15.00 items brought in $35.00 of sales.

It might not always be possible, depending on your product, to offer additions to your product, but ask friends and family if they can think of related products.  Jewelry is often easiest, as you can design earrings to match with necklaces, etc.  Photographers often sell frames.  Many doll makers will offer 'accessories'.  One of the cutest I saw was a pair of rabbit ears that you could add to your teddy bear.  I could easily imagine an entire line of ears and horns that could go with the bears!  Customers who had previously bought the teddy bears could come and buy these little extras.

And of course, another way is always selling more of your product, by offering a select discount on multiple purchases.

# **<u>Beware the Discount</u>**

I honestly think that overall discounts, or 'on-sale' items at a craft show can create more problems than they solve. Perhaps, for some vendors, they might lead to more sales. But I have seen too many vendors lose money on 'sale' merchandise.

When you present your work as unique or special, a discounted area suggests that these particular items are not as special as everything else. Maybe they are old stock, out of fashion, or more cheaply made than the rest of your items. People often want to know *why* something is on sale.

Think carefully before you offer any blanket discounts. Some vendors have a small section with signs that say, "SALE" or "BOGO - Buy One Get One". It can tend to draw people who are looking only for discounts. You aren't a bargain store. You are an craftsperson. You've worked out your pricing, and tried your best to come up with a fair figure.

Now, I do offer some discounts. I discount under the following 3 circumstances:

1. When someone is honestly short on the cash and really want the item. This usually involves someone who goes through their pockets, counts all the change they have and realizes they are a dollar or two short. I've been there, and so I feel the pain.

2. I have a small group of customers who I know - and I offer

them discounts on any items they buy.  They are familiar faces.  They've spent hundreds of dollars and they get special pricing.  I offer them a discount because I appreciate their business.

3. I do offer to discount multiple purchases.  Although I primary create necklaces, I will point out earrings and offer a tempting price for the 'set'.

I usually don't push the sale, but will mention the discount if they appear to be looking at a second product or are having problems choosing between two items.

Since I know my product price and mark-up well, I also offer my discounts in 2 stages.  Stage one is where I offer a smaller discount and then depending on the reaction, I will proceed to a steeper discount.

Here's a scenario:

Oliver's customer is considering buying two of his sock monkeys.  One is $35 and one is $45.  He suggests, "If you can't decide between them, I can give you $5.00 off the bigger monkey if you buy the little guy."

And here's the trick for offering these types of discounts: After you've presented the discount you stop talking.  Just. Stop. Talking.  It gives your customer time to think and assess their budget.  Oliver will get some feedback - even non-verbal (a frown, a narrowing of their eyes, a nod or a big sigh).

"Sigh," says the customer.

After a few seconds of continued silence, Oliver says, "I know, it's a tough choice.  (pause) How about $70 for them both?".

Oliver has offered the discount in two stages. If he went straight to the $70 price, he would have no room to lower it. It is also possible that the customer is fine with a $5 discount. Pausing before speaking also indicates that he is considering his pricing and the offer.

Chances are good the 2nd price would be enough of a discount to tempt this customer. He shouldn't go any lower, because he'd be selling at a loss or at the break-even point. If he goes too much lower, it also makes people wonder about his original prices.

You have to stress that the discount applies for both items. If Oliver had said, "If you get them both, it's like $30 for the little guy and $40 for the bigger one.", he will be opening himself up to the customer saying, "How about $30 for the small monkey?" and walking off with just one item. I've seen it happen frequently, and put myself into that same situation, so now I'm a bit more cautious.

Remember, discounts come straight out of your profits. You've worked hard on your products, and at your pricing. If you are offering a fair price, then you aren't obligated to discount your work at all.

# **Observation and Interaction**

Once someone has 'entered your space' or approached your table, give them a moment to look at your product. I always think of it as giving people 'room to breathe'. Some vendors will immediately start telling a person about their product but most people need a few seconds to process what they are viewing.

Use those few seconds to see what catches their attention. Are they drawn to a item? Have the stopped at a particular area, or are they reading the prices or information?

If nothing seems to catch their attention, or they are about to pass by without looking at your work, then take a minute to bring some special feature to their attention. I will often pick up one of my robot sculptures and tell them, "this is made from a vintage vacuum tube". If they are familiar with vacuum tubes, they will usually tell me, and if they aren't - this is the chance to present the product.

What happens if you are shy? Not every vendor is an extrovert, and it can be tough to talk to strangers. Ask a question!

Asking open ended questions is always a good way to engage people. Questions that lead to yes or no answers can lead to dead end conversations. "Are you looking for something for someone special?" can be answered by a quick "No", and a rapid exit. Genuine interest goes a long way.

If you are stuck trying to think of some way to engage them, try asking questions like, "What do you think of the craft show so far?", or "What else have you seen at the show?". I'm often extremely interested in their responses because I'm trapped at my table and unable to wander around. I really do want to know what they think of the show.

Listen carefully and don't interrupt.

Occasionally someone will enter my space and immediately say "Oh, I'm just looking!". It's often an automatic response, like saying ouch when you are burned. I know I can get a bit defensive when I walk into a store, and I've blurted out the 'just looking' line automatically. I once said that to a sales person and she replied, "Let me know if you find any money!", and it made me laugh.

When someone tells me they are "just looking", I usually reply, "Oh, there is just so much to see here." Depending on the person's body language I might just nod a response, or smile.

Some people are simply browsing, wasting time or uninterested in your product. Maybe they're exhausted by hearing a pitch from the next booth. Whatever their reason it's a 'give me some space' cue that you shouldn't ignore.

That will all change if they touch something...

# Place it in Their Hands

Once a person moves beyond the visual appeal of your product they will often reach out and touch.  This is a time for action.

The moment when someone touches one of your products they are showing greater interest.  Curiosity is being expressed and it is an opportunity to engage the person.  I will often take a necklace off the display and place it in their hands.  You can do this subtly by pointing out some of those key features, "this wool is very soft", "isn't it lightweight?".

The act of holding an item can trigger some primal instincts that go beyond mere feel.  When someone feels how soft and cuddly Oliver's sock monkeys are, more than their eyes are captivated.

We've all heard the expression, 'possession is nine-tenths of the law', and often the act of holding an object creates a sense of ownership.  This is especially evident if the item is unique.  I've seen this countless times when someone has picked up an item, put it down, and then sees someone else pick up that same item.  The first person immediately wants it in a, "This is Mine! You can't have it!", playground response.

The longer someone holds onto an item the more likely they are to buy it.  This does not mean, though, that you are guaranteed a sale, but there is a much better chance of closing a transaction.

# PART 7:  Technology

Craft shows have changed over the years and some of the new technology is a challenge for some vendors.  Not everyone loves it, but it is available, and often useful.

So how can you make technology work for you at your shows?

# Accept all forms of Payment

Cash? Yes. PayPal? Yes. Credit Cards, rolled coins, the change in your pocket, money borrowed from Mom? Yes! As my old boss Max would say: it is better to walk away with something in your pocket then to go home with nothing.

Now with changes and advances in technology, people have a lot more options to pay for your hand crafted items. If you only accept cash you are limiting your potential sales.

New options like the credit card reader, SQUARE , allow small vendors to accept credit cards at more reasonable rates. You will need a smart phone, so don't forget to factor that into your costs. One benefit to using SQUARE is that there are no monthly fees and the money you earn is deposited quickly into your bank account - usually the next day. About 20% of my sales are now done with credit cards. Some vendors I know haven't made any sales with these devices, but since it doesn't cost them anything to own (they ship you the reader for free), it's offers them an advantage.

Review the different payment options and accept as many as you can.

Cash and credit cards are the most popular, but I've accepted bank transfers, foreign currency (at a reduced exchange rate), and Pay Pal. With a smart phone I was able to see immediately that I received a Pay Pal transfer.

On occasion I have taken checks, but these have become rare. In the past ten years I've only had two checks, both from older buyers.

Don't let the fact someone doesn't have enough cash or doesn't have a credit card stand between you and your sale. A deposit now on 'Layaway' for future pick-up can work too.

# The Social Media Circus

Do you have a Facebook business page or a Twitter account? What about a blog or a personal website? Instagram, Pinterest, a DeviantArt page, Flickr? There are hundreds of ways you can be online, and most of them can help but the options are overwhelming and time consuming.

Which one is best? The one your customers expect. Currently, this means you should have at least a small Facebook page.

I get overwhelmed by all the virtual options, so I've focused my efforts on two popular choices: Facebook and Twitter. I still update some of the other accounts but far less frequently. My Facebook and Twitter accounts usually have a few posts that let people know what new projects I have on the go, what shows I plan on doing, and any new listings I have on Etsy.

Focus on the accounts you can effectively manage. There are certain tools that can assist you in updating like HootSuite (www.hootsuite.com), which allow you to schedule posts and tweets.

And once you've figured out which of these circus sideshows you will attend - don't forget to post about your next Show! Tell your friends and followers when you are confirmed for the show, post them another time, about two weeks before the show, again a few days before - and on the day of the show.

# A Special Note about Facebook

A good friend of mine runs a very successful Facebook page with lots of entertaining posts, glimpses into his personal life, photos and his art.  He updates his account a few times a week or more, and he doesn't spend all his time flogging his art.  He is always genuine.  I always loved his posts even when there was just a few hundred followers.  One day his work was discovered by a local celebrity, and then it was picked up by a few blogs.  When his work was purchased by a famous person, his number of followers went up 100 times, and his sales went through the roof.

We've all read similar stories of being discovered, but the most important part of these stories is that you could find my friend online.  If he hadn't had an online store, a Twitter and Facebook account, there would have been no way to reach him outside of his personal email.

When vendors tell me they don't have a Facebook page, I wonder how their customers find out about their shows.  More and more shows are now organized and advertised via Facebook.

In the fall of 2014, Etsy.com organized craft shows in many cities across North America.  They set up local pages for each of the shows and encouraged vendors to invite people.  Thousands of invitations went out on Facebook and it was one of the most successful events I have experienced.

So do you need a Facebook page? I would suggest it, even if

you don't end up getting a lot of followers, simply because it is a very popular avenue for customers to find you.

One day something better will come along - and Facebook may go the way of the dinosaur or it may not - but until then, take it under consideration.

An important thing to remember is that Facebook will push you towards buying advertisements and getting more followers. In 2015 there have been some noticeable changes in the way your pages might get displayed on various feeds. This has resulted in some page displaying less frequently, and becoming harder to find. It means that for small businesses a Facebook page might not be as accessible as it was before - but it also is still yet another way for your customers to find you.

# E-mail Lists

For a year or two I've had a sheet (if there is space at the table) labeled "Mailing List". I only send two or three bulk emails a year, usually letting them know about shows I will be attending, if there are any changes with my products, (items going out of stock, price changes, new product lines), and any new websites or places to find me.

No one likes a lot of spam, and if you are sending an e-mail a week about some sale or promotion - a lot of people will delete those emails.

If you want to see what kind of result your e-mails generate, using a product like MAIL CHIMP. This will allow you to see if your e-mail has been opened. If you have links to your site you can see how many people clicked on the link. Links are most successful if they go to a part of your site that might allow a customer to see the list of shows or if they offer a print out for a coupon.

## Become Accessible

Recently I was a bit shocked to get a business card from a vendor that only had her phone number and business name. She didn't want to give out her e-mail address. The chance of me contacting her dropped to nearly zero. Later she wrote her personal e-mail on the back of her card.

Your customers expect your e-mail address, and also expect you to respond to their e-mails.

I have seen the opposite problem. Instead of a lack of an e-mail address, someone has listed 1001 ways to contact them. Their cards are crowded with addresses from their Pinterest boards, variations of Twitter, Instagram, Flickr, Deviant Art, and any other page associated with their company.

List only a chosen few sites and one e-mail address. It is a bit like an over-crowded display: when people don't know where to start they will frequently walk away.

Whatever you chose, just make sure someone can reach you. E-mail addresses, websites, and your telephone number are the top choices. At this time, Facebook and to a lesser degree, Twitter, are your next options to review.

# iPads and Tablet Displays

Do you have good photos of your work? A tablet with product photos - running as a slide show can grab attention. If you can't captivate them with a video - a slide show is a great option.

Slide shows on your iPad or tablet should show the products you have for sale or available on a commission basis. Most of my necklaces are unique, so I will use photos with models from photo shoots or magazines. These photos allow the viewer to see how the jewelry looks without looking at the specific piece. I will intersperse these photos with a few shots of older items that are similar to what I have available.

Macro photos tend to work very well, because they show off aspects of your design that might not be apparent at first glance. One vendor I know will show off the buttons used in her work and macro photos of her hand sewn finished edges.

A slide show of photos can catch the attention of people who might be a bit shy to speak to you, and it can also stir a lot of interest. People tend to respond and watch things that move, and it is a good, simple way to add another captivating aspect to your booth or table.

Another great thing: iPads or a tablet can double as a camera or mirror in a pinch!

## PART 8:  The Odds and Ends

Well, we're finally near the end of the book.  The next section are more tips and ideas that didn't fit quite so neatly into the previous sections:

# Layaway Sales

Once in a while, I've had customers ask me to put items aside. Usually I will tell them I can hold it for an hour. About 30% of my customers return to purchase the item but many vanish never to be seen again. Very rarely someone will come back and tell me they aren't going to purchase it, or that they picked out something else.

Some customers will ask me to do a layaway until they have the money. I usually ask for a deposit, get their e-mail or cell phone number, and make certain they have mine. I suggest you also set an approximate "Sell by" date, so in 5 or 6 weeks if they haven't contacted you, then you tell them you will sell it.

So if someone didn't pick up the item they put on layaway, what happens to the deposit? Well, that is up to you. I've never kept those deposits if I can reach the person. I've sent deposits back via Pay Pal if necessary. Some vendors do keep the deposit, but I don't.

Whatever your policy on setting something aside, or taking a deposit, make sure both you and your customers clearly understand the details.

## <u>Keep Show Notes</u>

Bring a notebook wherein: you can finalize sales tallies, make notes about the number of sales you made at the show, how many people took business cards, the weather and general observations.  This allows you to not only track what shows are popular, but determine if you are choosing the right type of show for your product.   Some shows might be well advertised but the crowd turn out is poor due to weather, construction or even a lack of signage.  I once did a show that turned out to be in the basement of a local store.  Although it was well advertised the location was confusing, and the few customers that braved the stairs looked shocked that there was a small room full of crafters hidden away.

I use a scale rating system for the shows, with 10 being the highest, that judge the show results.  At the end of the book I'm going to provide a few ideas you can use to help you keep track of the shows, and how you did with them.  I'll put an example of my personal "Show Note Form" at the end of this book.

# **Presentation and Packaging**

Many customers come to Craft Shows searching for gifts. It can be annoying if they buy something from you and then have to spend a week finding a box to fit the pottery they bought.

What can be more annoying is buying something and then finding out that the vendor has run out of bags or boxes. It happened to me a few times when I didn't bother to bring enough boxes (or bags) for my items, because I didn't think I would sell as much as I did. 20 necklaces, 10 boxes. What was I thinking?

Most of my goods are presented to the customer in boxes. Before I put the lid on the item, I will show them their purchase. This helps confirm the sale (yes, this is what they bought), but also makes you look professional.

Good packaging makes for good presentation. I buy what I can afford in bulk. One day I'd love to design special boxes for the robots, but for now simple bulk boxes will do.

## **Don't Ask Other Vendors About their Sales**

I don't think I've ever had anyone talk to me about their actual hard stats for their sales at a show, at least until I've known the vendor for years. Most of the time it makes people uncomfortable. If they suspect they have done better then you, they worry you might resent them. If they find out you are doing better - they might feel resentful or question their own work. Pretty much everyone hates discussing their sales.

# Don't do it all Alone

For me it can be difficult to resist doing everything myself. I am a fairly competent photographer, graphics creator, and I tend towards trying to do everything. If I need a layout for some print media - say a brochure - the first thing I do is to start learning brochure layouts. Sometimes I even figure out that I actually can't to do layouts, or I don't have the right programs.

At that point I will often back away from the new project - or pay a professional.

If you are very lucky, you can find someone to help you without paying them. That might work once or twice but eventually you can run out of favors. Maybe you can trade your skills or art for better photos to use on your website.

I found one of the best things to do is just ask people for help. Solicit their advice. "Great business card! Who did the design?" can open a lot of doors and provide you with more information.

As well, there may be some shows where you will need sales help. Although I've hired many assistants over the years, very few of them were really compatible, and fewer yet were sales people. If you can find a few good sales people, hang on to them. I always try and pay any helpers well, and give them a bonus if we have a great day.

# <u>Reward Yourself</u>

Whether I have had a good or a poor show, I always try and have some little reward at the end. If it was a poor show it might just be pizza for dinner, or a really good latte the next day. My husband is always hoping it will be a spectacular show - so that we will go to one of our favorite restaurants.

If you have helpers, or have hired assistants for the show, even if you haven't sold a lot - make sure to allot something as a bonus. A gift, a thank you card, or something. Appreciation goes a long way.

Not all rewards are about money, though a pile of cash makes everyone happy.

Look for the benefits beyond the money. Did you get some fantastic feedback? Did you meet an interesting vendor, or brighten some customer's day? Did you feed your supporters lots of pizza? Finding some inspiration always makes me very happy.

# **Thank your Supporters**

Every time someone has purchased something they are directly showing you their support. Take a minute and let them know how much it means to you.

I'm truly grateful to the people who buy my work, or e-mail me, or just spend a minute saying something nice. Even just a Tweet can really make me smile.

Don't forget to thank the organizers. Even if the show was not a huge success, thank them.

Writing this book has been a lot of fun, and I'd love to hear what you think, so in some future year, when I'm releasing a Second Edition, it will be even better.

So, here's a thanks to all of you: readers, my fellow vendors, my friends, supporters and acquaintances.

## <u>Final Words</u>

After all this serious stuff, the tips and tricks... the important thing is that Craft Shows can still be FUN. You will get to meet new people, talk to fellow creative folks, see new ideas, and meet supporters.

HAVE FUN!

Don't forget to check the Appendix for the Show Notes and your Check List. Both the Show Notes and the Check List can also be obtained Electronically - in Word format. I will post the URL on my Facebook and let you know the details, or you can check the website: www.finaldraftpress.com

## Acknowledgements:

I'd like to thank my husband, who has supported me over the years, listened to my madness, schemed with me, and endured. He tells me to have fun and plays me a theme song when I leave for a show.

Special thanks to Cinnabari, my virtual sister-in-arms, who constantly reminds me of the difference between "then" and "than". To my friend Regan, who also has endured a decade of writing discussions. We will make this work!

Thanks to William J. Smith for the editing and immoral support. Love to Mom, that creative free spirit, and Dad who taught me how to make jewelry.

You can find me: facebook.com/ClockworkZero

Or email me via Final Draft Press' (the publishing company) at: clockworkzero@finaldraftpress.com

# Appendix

**Craft Show Checklist**

**Show Notes**

## CRAFTSHOW CHECKLIST

**Show Name:**                    **Date:**

**Address:**                    **Set up Time:**

**Organizer Contact Info:**

### Craft Show Box/Bag

- [ ] Tablecloth
- [ ] Scissors
- [ ] Masking / Duct Tape
- [ ] Clear tape
- [ ] Notebook
- [ ] magnifying glass
- [ ] mirror
- [ ] Calculator
- [ ] Receipt Book
- [ ] Glue
- [ ] Pen
- [ ] Plastic Bags
- [ ] Safety pins
- [ ] Mints
- [ ] Cash box/wallet
- [ ] Signs / Banner
- [ ] Price Tags
- [ ] Lint Roller

### Stock Items

- [ ] Gift Boxes
- [ ] Gift Bags
- [ ] Tissue Paper
- [ ] Mailing list sign-up sheet
- [ ] Business Cards
- [ ] Bubble Wrap

### Equipment

- [ ] Camera
- [ ] iPad
- [ ] Tools
- [ ] Phone
- [ ] Credit Card Reader
- [ ] Lighting

### Perishables

- [ ] Food
- [ ] Snacks /Energy Bars
- [ ] Water / Energy Drink

## EXTRAS

- ☐ Thick Work-out Mat to stand on
- ☐ Folding Chair
- ☐ Flyers
- ☐ Medication
- ☐ Elastics
- ☐ Binder clips
- ☐ Phone charger

- ☐ Power bars
- ☐ Kleenex
- ☐ Hand Sanitizer
- ☐ Gift Certificates
- ☐ Extra Pen
- ☐ Lip Balm
- ☐ Paper Towels
- ☐ Wet Naps
- ☐ Deodorant

**OUTDOOR SHOW**
**Additional items**

☐ Folding Chair

☐ Folding Tables

☐ Tent

☐ Sunscreen

☐ Tent Pegs

☐ Hammer

☐ Trash bags

☐ Extra Shoes

☐ Jacket

☐ Umbrella

☐ Banner

☐ Cash Box

☐ Twine

☐ Screwdriver

☐ Plastic boxes

☐ Dolly

☐ Bug Repellant

☐ Allergy Meds

☐ Hat

☐ Outdoor First Aid

## Show Notes

**Show Name:**                    **Date:**

**Organizer Contact Info:**

**Fee / Costs:**

**Float:  $**

**Annual show?      Y   N**

**Table required?   Y   N**

**Chairs required?  Y   N**

**Where did you find out about the show:**

**Rate each of the following using a scale of 1-10 (lowest to highest):**

**Advertising:**            _____

**Attendance:**            _____

**Organization:**          _____

**Weather:**                _____

**Location:**                _____

**Number of items sold:** _____

**Total Sales in Dollars:** _____

**Apply again?   Y   N   Maybe**

**Comments:**

# ABOUT THE AUTHOR

Colleen Manestar is a geek girl, who did a long stint in tech support. She's a writer, a photographer, an artisan and can cook up a storm. She's married and has a cat. She's known as C.A. Manestar, Zero, clockworkzero and occasionally, Colleen. She's had a few short science fiction, horror stories published here and there.